The
Big Spark

Instant Action Steps
To Spark Your
Business

T. Ray Greer, Jr.

ISBN: **1517290767**
ISBN-13: **978-1517290764**

DEDICATION

Do you remember when you were young? When you were young you trusted that you could do anything but fail. Well, you're older now and a lot has changed since your youth. However, I hope one thing hasn't changed at all. I hope you still believe in you. If you don't believe in you just consider this one fact, I believe in you! In fact, I wrote this book because of my confidence in you. I dedicate this book to all the entrepreneurs who aren't afraid to dream.

CONTENTS

CONNECT WITH ME!

www.facebook.com/THEWORLDOFGREEROLOGY
www.youtube.com/user/GREEROLOGY
Periscope: @TRAYGREERJR
www.GREEROLOGY.org
Twitter: @RAYGREER

Please download the app, Greerology, on Google Play, Apple Store and Amazon today!

"Don't count every hour in the day, make every hour in the day count."
~**Anonymous**

Life is created by a series of events. If you can find some way to pull 20 extra minutes out of your life, you'd better use them wisely. Where will you discover this time, and when you find this time, how will you use it?

Just 20 minutes a day will convert into a powerful 121 hours a year. That is a huge piece of time that you can use to gain new capacities and expand. The advantage is seen when we make a day by day inclination and submit those 20 minutes to something beneficial. You can awaken 20 minutes before, take 20 minutes from lunch, after work, or just before bed — the decision is totally up to you. Just do it! Remove all excuses and distractions.

Secondly, you need a strategy that connects you with your target audience! The strategy has to connect you to your clients and prospects aggressively. The most dazzling strategy won't help you earn a revenue or accomplish your unbelievable dreams if it isn't built around your target audience. A strategy that isn't based on customers is rather like a man who knows a thousand ways to fish, but doesn't know where any fishing spots are located. Great in notion but fruitless in results. Can I show you where the spots are located to spark your business?

As Shakespeare said, "Action is eloquence". So let's add some eloquence to your business right now! It doesn't matter if you been in business 20 years or you have just came up with a possible business 20 minutes ago, promote it starting now!

Before you invest all your money in a new venture, become a smart marketer. Take time at the beginning to discover who your potential customers are, and how to effectively reach them.

Without a plan, your entrepreneurial dream is really wishful thinking. While a marketing plan can be a map for success, remember that the map is not the territory. A strategy that ignores the customer isn't an accurate reflection of the landscape.

A good marketing plan can help you focus your energy and resources. But a plan created in a vacuum, based solely on your perceptions, does not advance the agenda. That's why market research, however simple or sophisticated, is important.

Just keep in mind that research attempts to predict the future by studying the past. It reveals what people have done, and extrapolates what people *might* do — not what people *will* do.

Planning is imperative, research is important, but there's no substitute for entrepreneurial insight. After all, as Mark Twain wrote, "You cannot depend on your eyes when your imagination is out of focus".

Promotion isn't something that ought to be done randomly, just when you think you have sufficient energy to do it. Honestly, as an entrepreneur who's always busy, you're never going to have room schedule-wise. Consequently, you need to make time for what's important. This implies doing something intentional each and every day. Before you think you don't have room schedule-wise to do that, reconsider. Showcasing doesn't need to be hours of your day. Instead, it's something you can do in as little time as 20 minutes a day.

Vilfredo Pareto introduced in the 1790s the "Pareto Principle," which believes that 20 percent of our efforts produce 80 percent of our results. Don't underestimate the power of 20.

1

SPARK

A small particle of a burning substance thrown out by a body in combustion created by friction.

1. Customer relations. This may not appear like a tip for advertising your business however it's totally still the best one of all times. Consider it - if a client or potential customer mention your name on any social media platform, you now have the chance to open up some serious conversation with them (and their followers/friends as well!). Also, you can do this all inside of 20 minutes a day! When you're taking care of client administration by means of email messages, verify you have an email signature that has your business data recorded in the mark. Incorporate a connection to your site, contact data and you can even welcome them to connect with you on social media platforms.

2. Experience the power of Periscope. Take 20 minutes a day and experience Periscope. Periscope is already proving to be an incredibly powerful social tool, and savvy marketers are using it in innovative ways to grow their businesses. Simply put, Periscope enables you to "go live" via your mobile device anytime and anywhere. The app enables you to become your own "on the go" broadcasting station, streaming video and audio to any viewers who join your broadcast.

Keep reading because you will discover powerful tools by using Periscope to empower your business.

3. Date your blog. Take 20 minutes a day and look at your blog numbers. It's critical to know data, for example, what decisive words are being utilized to discover your site, what page is being seen the most, and that's just the beginning. Dating your blog gives you inside data into precisely what your business needs. And after that it's dependent upon you to offer it to them by making considerably more powerful content predicated on what you're learned from your research. This simple action will guarantee that you're furnishing them with great substance that you know they will need at some point.

4. Connect with a marketing blog. Lay aside 20 minutes to peruse a current marketing blog or article. Be that as it may, take some extra steps than simply reading them. Leave 2-3 minutes so you can comments on the blog. There are two reasons for doing this. One, you'll be advertising your business in light of the fact that you'll have the capacity to incorporate a connection to your business in the remark. Two, it likewise gets your name before different advertisers (this is particularly imperative in case you're remarking on content that has a place with huge influencers in your particular specialty). What's more, bear in mind to bookmark the site so you can check it every day.

5. Become a member of an online forum. Set aside some an opportunity to investigate diverse online discussions. Discover one where your target audience congregate together and join the discussion. Most online groups will give you a chance to include a signature line. Utilize this space to add a connection to your site, your name/business name. At that point invest energy every day going to the gathering and connecting with clients and prospects.

6. Pinterest. Sign up for a free Pinterest account and quickly edit the profile data to incorporate a connection to your site, a brief business depiction, picture of yourself and that's just the beginning. Now this is an extraordinary approach to advertising your business. Pinterest is similar to a major announcement board where you get the chance to pin whatever you want to. This way you can let your audience become more acquainted with you. You can create a board with your favorite teams, players, cites and that's only the tip of the iceberg. Be that as it may, keep in mind to make a business board where you can showcase your business by posting related information, items you're offering, and so forth. Bear in mind, it's likewise about cooperating with different pinners too – leave a remark on a pin they shared, re-pin something they shared. Be creative and intentional.

7. Facebook. This is another online networking opportunity that you can't afford to miss. Set aside the opportunity to set up a page for your business so you can keep it isolate from your own personal profile. After you've made the page, add a couple of posts on it before you begin searching for others to like your page. Remember to promote your page as well as promote other businesses are well.

The 20 minutes a day you spend on Facebook ought to be more about building associations with your followers, not about self-advancement. Remember individuals purchase from those they know, and trust. Facebook is an incredible spot for clients and potential clients to become acquainted with you! Offer profitable data that is associated with them and they'll continue to return.

8. Twitter. Here's another online networking platform that gives you a free promotional platform. When you make your Twitter account, edit the profile and add a link to your site. Also, add a brief (you just get 160 characters) portrayal about you/your business. At that point begin uniting with individuals like your clients, potential clients, your rivals and your cluster of experts in your general range, and so on.

Spend your 20 minutes a day carefully. At the outset it's a smart thought to invest this energy discovering individuals to unite with and collaborate with them. Rather than simply tailing somebody, why not send a Tweet to them. Something like "hey @username, incredible slogan (photograph, blog entry, whatever). Anticipating them following you." Engage with them, Retweet their stuff. When you Tweet, keep in mind to keep the advertising/special stuff to a minimum.

9. LinkedIn. Going along with the social media theme, LinkedIn is another platform you can market your business for free. Like Facebook, they also now include business pages. Unlike Facebook where anyone can set up a FB page, there are some requirements your personal LinkedIn profile must reach first before you're eligible for a business page. Read those here: (https://help.linkedin.com/app/answers/detail/a_id/1594/ft/eng). But your personal profile will work just fine. Once you have an account set up, edit it to include a description about your business, a link to your website, your skills, etc. Spend your 20 minutes a day participating in some LinkedIn groups. Comment on posts, answer questions, etc. Groups are a great way to find people to connect with and add them to your connections (LinkedIn calls them connections not friends).

10. Google+. Google+ has what's called a hover card. When someone hovers over your name this card pops up. In the screenshot to the right, you can see the hover card in action. The text is small but it says:

Obsessive Social Media Trailblazer, Facebook Marketing & Relationship Marketing Speaker and Author MariSmith.com • Social Media Consultant, Trainer & Speaker • Facebook Marketing Expert • Author, 'The New Relationship Marketing' • Coauthor: 'Facebook Marketing: An Hour A Day' • Named one of the Top Ten Social Media Influencers by D&B Credibility and Forbes • Dubbed 'The pied piper of the online world' by Fast Company • Scottish-Canadian ツ San Diego, California

And then there's the box giving you the option to add her to your circles. All that to say, use your 20 minutes a day commenting on posts. Why? Because when you do, people will be able to hover over your name and see more details about you. This is a great way to start interacting with others and marketing your business in a relationship building sort of way!

11. Return on Investment. Now that we just covered a bunch of social media ideas for marketing your business, it's important that you spend time tracking your efforts. You have to know what the ROI (return on investment) is that you're getting. If you find that you're not getting any interaction or traffic from your Pinterest efforts, then maybe you need to stop focusing on that one and instead focus where you are seeing the most ROI. Part of marketing your business every day, is knowing where/how to best spend those 20 minutes a day.

12. Live event Q&A sessions. If you're at a live event most of them offer Q&A sessions after a speaker/session. Take the time to ask a relevant question. Why? These are usually recorded and before you ask your question you can say your name and your website URL. Quick and easy way to market your business. Those in the room with you will now know who you are/what your website URL is and anyone that purchases the recordings and listens at a later date will hear the same info.

13. Attend live webinars. This is another way to market your business quickly and easily, not necessarily in 20 minutes a day, but still worth your marketing efforts. During the Q&A session (most webinar presenters always provide a time for questions) chime in. If you have the opportunity to 'take the microphone' and talk, do this because your name and URL will be said out loud and the recording will pick it up. Sometimes, if you put a question in the chat section, a webinar presenter will state your name/URL but it's better if you can say it, so it's pronounced properly.

14. Facebook ads. When it comes to marketing your business to a very targeted group of people, Facebook ads is one possible choice. They're great for a special product, time-limited item, or even a free webinar. You can also use them to get more likes. Whatever you decide when it comes to Facebook ads, keep in mind that you have to have a goal you want to achieve. And then don't forget to include a very clear call to action – people have to know exactly what you want them to do when they see this ad

15. Recycle old content. Set aside 20 minutes a day to go through your old content. Find ways to repurpose it. Maybe that means you rewrite it, create videos, write a report to go with it, record a podcast episode – it doesn't matter, just do something with it so that you can use it to market your business.

16. Distribute old content on social media. All that old content that was just mentioned, aside from recycling it into fresh, new content, you can still use it to market your business. Each day take time to share some of the old stuff on social media. Maybe focus on one piece of content each day. When doing this, just remember to tweak things a little when posting to your different social media sites so that followers, who are connected with you in more than one place, aren't seeing the same thing on each site.

17. Blog. Blogging is going to be one of the most essential parts of your marketing plan – and if it's not, it should be. Your blog is your main hub on the Internet and the only way to get visitors there and to keep your content current. Now it may take you longer than 20 minutes to write a blog post, but imagine what you could do if you schedule regular blocks of time on your calendar to do this. In addition to creating your own content, another option (and this should only take you 20 or less minutes) is what's known as content curating. This simply means finding something you think is share worthy and valuable to your audience and you write a brief post about it, quote something from the content you're sharing and then link to the other site.

18. Handout business cards. Only you can decide if this is a marketing tactic you want to spend 20 minutes a day doing. If you don't target local businesses, it might not make sense to do this every day. But whatever works for you, handing out business cards is a great way to market your business. When you're in line at the grocery store, start a conversation with the person by you;

leave cards on bulletin boards; remind others to pass them along to anyone who might be helped by your services or products.

19. Car magnet or decal. Speaking of going out in public and handing out business cards, why not use your car as a big business card? Have a magnet sign with your name, business name, website link and contact information. This is a great way to market your business over and over without you having to do anything other than stick the magnet or decal on your car.

20. Google Alerts. There's more to Google alerts than just knowing when people mention your name or business. You can set up these alerts to notify you every day about a specific keyword, keyword phrase or name that you want to keep an eye on in your market. These alerts can be used to generate content ideas, show you where to post a comment (if it's a blog post or article), and more. Google alerts are also a great way to monitor your online reputation. Whether people are saying something positive or negative about you, it gives you a chance to go and interact with them.

2

INCIPIENT

When heat, oxygen and a fuel source combine to have a chemical reaction resulting in a fire. This is also known as "ignition" and is usually generated by a spark.

21. Reach out to past customers. Take a few minutes each day to craft an email message letting former clients know you miss them. A great time to reach out to them is if you are releasing a new product or have a new service available. Don't be afraid to take it a step further and make things even more personable, too. If you have their phone number, pick up the phone and call them. More than likely you won't be bothering them, they'll be tickled that you went above and beyond normal customer service and took the time to reach them on the phone.

22. Word of mouth referrals from current customers. Get others to market for you! As a consumer, you know that whether you have a good or bad experience with someone (or a store, restaurant or other business) you're likely to talk about it. This is even more so in this day and age with easy access to social media sites like Facebook, Instagram, Twitter, and more. So let your satisfied customers do the marketing for you by giving word of mouth referrals, testimonials and social media shout outs. Give them an incentive to spread the word – maybe offer a referral fee if you're a service provider or an affiliate commission if you sell products.

23. Reach out to potential clients and customers. Reach out to your target audience – those potential clients and customers you would love to have as a customer. You can do this in 20 minutes a day by finding their websites, forums they hang out in and social media groups they're a part of. Once you know where they are, take 20 minutes every day and visit those places. Don't just lurk though. You can't market yourself if you're not interacting. Take an interest in them, their problems and things they share. Take the time to answer their questions and offer assistance where you can. You have to show them there's a reason to visit your site/buy your product/work with you.

24. Email marketing. Don't forget another one of the most important marketing tips there is – email marketing. It's important to always be actively working on building your mailing list and mailing them on a consistent basis. Putting yourself in front of your subscribers regularly helps them remember who you are. And also gives you the opportunity to market your services, products, affiliate products, share great content and more.

25. Connect with the "big guys" in your industry. Spending 20 minutes a day researching the big influencers in your industry can lead to some huge opportunities for you in the future. Of course, it's not just a matter of researching them and finding out who they are and where they hang out. It's important that you take the time to start interacting with them, too. A great place to start is by signing up for their mailing list. Then connect with them on social media sites. Once you have started building a relationship with them, you can reach out to them about the possibility of guest blogging for them or appearing as a guest on their podcast, etc. Whatever you do, don't reach out to them without first knowing a bit about them and how they conduct their business so that when you approach them you can provide a win/win situation for the both of you.

26. Live tutorials on Periscope. It doesn't matter whether it's a new product for your customers, information on how to get the best from your best-selling app, or a training module for your personnel. There's no limit to the opportunities. Just 20 minutes could change your whole world.

27. Guest blog. There are a lot of marketers out there in the blogosphere who are happy to accept guest posts. Don't make the mistake of just approaching every Tom, Dick and Harry though. Instead, take the time to find relevant bloggers in your niche and then approach them. In just 20 minutes a day, you could email several of these bloggers with your pitch of a guest blog idea. Make sure it fits with the information they share with their audience. Once you get the go ahead to guest blog, create valuable, high-quality content. This is an excellent way to market yourself to a whole new audience that might not have found you otherwise.

28. Attend live events. This isn't something you can do in 15 minutes a day but it's still an important part of marketing your business. Live events mean you'll have to travel. Some are out of town and even require overnight (or several nights) stays. But don't discard this idea. Not only are they a way to get yourself out there in front of people you might have interacted with otherwise, they are the perfect opportunity to build relationships with others in your niche. You never know who you might meet at a live event. There are all sorts of possibilities with the different people you'll meet.

29. Host a webinar. There's no rule that says you have to host a 60 minute webinar, although most of them are. You can scale this back and do whatever works best for you. You'll need enough time to do what it is that you plan on using the webinar for. Example: if you are writing a new book, host a webinar to create some excitement about it. If you're launching (or just launched) a new product, host a webinar to tell people about it and maybe even give attendees a sweet deal on it. Webinars are the perfect way to deliver a powerful message and then throw a little marketing/promotion in at the end. Whatever you do, don't make the entire webinar a sales pitch. That's the quickest way to send people running for the hills!

30. Pitch yourself to podcast owners. Part of your 20 minutes a day marketing plan should also include researching possible podcast appearances you could make. Possible podcast owners to look for: your competitors, podcasts in your area of expertise or something that aligns with your expertise. Remember; don't just blindly pitch yourself to someone. Meaning, make sure you read through their guest guidelines and follow any rules they have before your pitch them. Put the time and effort into creating an effective pitch – something that makes you sound like someone they just have to interview.

31. Read a business book. Read a book every day for 16-18 minutes and then use the last couple minutes (of your 20 minutes) to share a gold nugget you picked up from the book. Post that gold nugget on all your social media platforms. Better yet, why not whip up a quick blog post about the book and then share a link to that post on social media.

32. Facebook likes. Today's 20 minutes could be used to go to your Facebook page and then find your favorite companies and like them. While you do not like them with an expectation that they'll like back, most people do. You could even spend a few minutes writing a post on their Facebook page about why you like them. Include a link back to your page and invite them to check you out.

33. Behind the scenes action on Periscope. You might be amazed at how attracted people are in a look behind the curtain of your business. Your crew building a home. Your graphic designers drafting a flyer. It's a great opportunity to get people involved with the story of your business. And the nature of Periscope makes it a great platform for a more informal look at your business for only 20 minutes.

34. HARO – help a reporter out. Sign up for HARO and then set aside 20 minutes a day to look through their emails. If you find something that might be a good fit and relevant place for you to market yourself, reach out to them. Follow the directions though! This is an excellent way to market yourself and potentially get some media coverage.

35. Keywords. While this isn't necessarily something you'll do 20 minutes every day, it plays a huge part in marketing your business. It's important that you spend time researching the terms people use to find the information and products you offer. You might not think this has anything to do with marketing your business but it has everything to do with it. Keywords are an essential part of your marketing plan because this is how you'll reach your target market. You must speak your prospects language at all times.

36. Submit a press release. If you're not a great copywriter, a press release may seem challenging to write. But don't throw this marketing idea out. You can always hire someone to write it for you and then you can spend your marketing time, submitting it and promoting it. This is a great way to market your business and also increase your credibility and visibility. It's pretty easy to submit to online directories but don't forget to also reach out to your local media outlets and see if they'll accept your press release too.

37. Offer open phones. For this tip, you'll need more than 20 minutes because each call you take should be about 20 minutes. This is an excellent way to market to potential customers by letting them call you with any questions they may have. Don't worry about closing a deal while on the call. Get their permission to send them a follow-up email and in that email you can summarize what you talked about and then mention a service or product you have that can help them.

38. Facebook Q&A session. Offer yourself for 20 minutes a day, at a specific time, so that people can post a question for you and you'll answer. Let your market know that you'll answer as many questions as possible within that 20 minute timeframe. Remind them, if you don't get to their question today, you'll be back again tomorrow. This is not only a great to market yourself, but it's an easy way to get your audience engaged with you!

39. Periscope Q&A session. Just like Facebook, Periscope would be an excellent platform for Q&A. Your audience would love to have 20 minutes of interaction with you through this channel. Always close your periscope with a call to action.

40. TED talks. These usually run about 18-20 minutes, so you may want to set aside 20 minutes every day to watch one of these. Choose from one of their 1800+ talks here (https://www.ted.com/talks). After you watch it, hop on over to your social media sites and share something you learned from it. Check out the speaker's bio for a link to their website and then see if they have any social media information on their site. If they do, follow them on Twitter, connect with them on Facebook. Check out their website too and see if they have a blog and if they do, skim through things and see if you can find any other information of theirs you might like to comment on or mention on social media.

3

GROWTH

This is where the fire load up and oxygen is used as fuel for the fire.

41. Research potential sponsorship opportunities both online and locally. Are there any events going on that your target market would be participating in? If so, contact the event organizer and see if they are looking for sponsors and if so what is the cost, etc. If it fits into your budget, sign up to sponsor it. If it's a live event, make sure you have business cards, flyers, and other marketing materials ready to go. If it's an online event, they'll probably list you as a sponsor and link back to your site

42. Google Adwords. This is an effective marketing strategy because it's a great way to get your business listed in search engines for specific keywords/keyword phrases. Make sure you take the time to research Google Adwords and familiarize yourself with how they work because if you don't, it can get expensive quick. One suggestion here is to set a monthly budget for this so you know what you have to work with.

43. Article marketing. Some people say article marketing is dead. Others still rely on it heavily as a way to market their business and increase their traffic. Only you will be able to tell if you're getting a good ROI on it. There are a lot of article submission directory sites out there, the most popular being Ezine

Articles. You'll have to narrow it down to a handful of sites or you could spend hours submitting articles.

44. Social Media Events. One thing that seems to go over really well on social media sites, specifically Facebook, is when you invite your audience to share links to their sites, or links to their pages. You've probably seen things like Fan Page Friday or Twitter Tuesday. These are ways for business owners to encourage their audience to interact with them and others. It also gives them promotion, which we're all looking for a little free promo now and then. Maybe you don't want to offer Fan Page Friday. Instead, maybe you want to offer your audience the opportunity to share a link of theirs every day. Maybe one day you could ask them to share a link to their favorite piece of content, a link to their favorite product, etc. You decide!

45. Respond to blog comments. If someone took the time to not only read your content, but actually write a comment about it, you better take the time to respond back. This shows that you value their time, that you do see the comments and respond back. It could also be a way to engage in a little conversation with a reader. When you respond back, maybe ask them a question – something that will get them to respond back to your response to them.

46. Google places. This won't take you 20 minutes a day, but listing your business on Google places is a great way to market your business for free. And because Google places is part of…well Google, its search engine will like this.

47. Yelp. Yelp has over 60 million users and over 20 million reviews posted (at time of writing). That says a lot about why you should have your business listed on their site. It may not need 20 minutes a day of your time, but it's worth setting up an account and getting your business listed. Your Yelp listing will help local people find your business. Make sure you take the time to respond to anyone who leaves a review about your business.

48. Visit your local library. Spend some time in their magazine section. Grab a magazine that you normally would never think of picking up and spend 20 minutes flipping through it. After you've done that, think about if you could create a blog post about something you learned that would benefit your audience. Or maybe it wasn't blog post worthy, but there was something you gleaned from it that would be worth at least putting a quick social media post up. Whatever you decide to do, go and do it.

49. Podcast. Start your own podcast. Maybe you won't do a podcast episode every single day, but when you do it, it can certainly be done in 20 minutes (or longer if you choose). Not only is this a marketing ploy, but it's also an excellent way to establish yourself as an expert.

50. Local media. You have to be a little cautious when pitching any media outlet – both online and offline. Before you pitch to your local media outlets, you have to decide whether or not you even have something newsworthy that is worth pitching. Do you offer something no one else does? Do you have a product or service that is trendsetting? These are just a few of the questions you can ask yourself in order to decide if something is worth pitching to the media.

51. Niche sites. Research some niche sites in your market. Once you find them, comment on their content, follow them on social media sites and start interacting. Share some of their content with your audience. The key is get them to notice you and then once you've started interacting with them, approach them to guest blog or have them guest blog, etc.

52. Publicity. Create a page on your website called 'in the media' or something along those lines. When you appear on a podcast, a media outlet references you, you guest post somewhere, or otherwise appear in public, be sure to add the information to your media page. Then it's time to start creating some social buzz about that publicity. Share it on social media. Ask friends to share it for you. Brag about yourself!

53. LinkedIn groups. There are a lot of groups on LinkedIn. Research them and find ones that are related to your niche. These groups will have your target audience hanging around. Show that you're an expert in your industry by answering questions and providing helpful information.

54. Facebook groups. Because anyone can quickly and easily create a Facebook group, you'll find them targeting just about everything you can think of. Spend some time researching groups and find a handful of ones that are niche specific and join them. Once you are added to the group make your presence known by commenting on things others posts, answering questions if you can, and providing value in other ways. The key is to stand out as an expert but do it in a way that isn't self-promotional or pushy.

55. Google hangouts. It's pretty simple to set up a Google hangout and broadcast live. This would be a great way to market your business by inviting potential customers to join you and ask you questions about your products and services. Let them get to know you while seeing your face and hearing your voice. If you're too "shy" to do a live hangout, you can do one with just yourself and then publish it to your website and invite people to view it there.

56. Group giveaways/partnerships. More than likely you've seen big group JV partnership events before where a group of people will get together and each of them will give away a product (or even sell it). If you have an opportunity to participate in something like this, it can be a good way to market your business. And a lot of times, the bigger benefit of doing something like this would be the opportunity to build your mailing list.

57. Stationery. Creating some notepads that have your business information on them is a fun way to market your business. Hand them out at a networking event, when you're out and about in public. Use them as thank you gifts for customers. Get creative – leave them at your local library, leave a few in the waiting room of your doctor's office.

58. Ask for product reviews. Research some bloggers in your market that could help get the word out about your product. Once you've compiled a decent sized list, start reaching out to them and finding out if they would be interested in reviewing your product in exchange for an honest review/testimonial of it.

59. Hashtag. It used to be that a hashtag (#) was only found on Twitter. Now, they've carried over into other social media platforms as well – Facebook and Instagram both use them, too. Create a hashtag for your business, a product, service, etc. and then when you're marketing on social media sites, be sure to use it. Let your customers and social media followers to use it too.

4

FULLY DEVELOPED

When the growth stage has reached its max and all combustible materials have been ignited. This is the hottest phase of a fire and the most dangerous.

60. Site directories. Add your site to some of the directories. A few of them that you can submit your site to are: Google (https://support.google.com/webmasters/answer/6259634) Bing, (http://www.bing.com/toolbox/submit-site-url) Link Directory, (http://www.linkdirectory.com/). There are a lot of other directories out there, but this is a good start. Note: some of these directories are free resources and others are paid resources.

61. Guest bloggers. Make a list of bloggers that would be a good fit for sharing content on your website. Start reaching out to them and find out if they would be interested in writing a guest post for you. Make sure that you provide them with a reason why that guest blogging for you would be worth their time and effort – do you get a large amount of traffic to your site, is your social media following large, etc. They need something to 'entice' them to put forth the effort to giving you content.

62. StumbleUpon. If you're not familiar with them, they're a social bookmarking site. Users add things to their profile based on what they like. It's an excellent way to drive more traffic to your online content and with 20 million users, there's a *potential* for your content to go viral. Top 10 (or other list type) posts tend to catch the eye of users, so keep this in mind and create some high quality, valuable list type posts for your blog. If you aren't interested in putting time into actively using StumbleUpon yourself and just want it for promotional purposes, they do have what's called Paid Discovery where you will pay 10 cents for every click through to your site. But why pay when you can spend just 20 minutes every day being an active StumbleUpon user instead?

63. Digg. Digg is just one more quick and easy way to market your business and get more traffic to your website. Submit your blog posts to Digg by entering the URL of it and a brief description. Make the description one that creates interest so people will want to digg it. Other people can also submit content for you – ask friends or others in your industry to submit something of yours and don't forget to return the favor!)

64. Social Monkee. This is a link building tool that you can use to create backlinks to your website. Every time you have new content on your site, submit it to Social Monkee. They'll then distribute it to up to 25 sites. They encourage you to spin the title and description of every submission you make. This is so that the backlinks don't all look the same.

65. Chamber of Commerce. Check out your local Chamber and find out about joining. This is an excellent way to not only get involved in your community, but it's a great way to market yourself locally. Once you join, attend the events and network. Anytime new members join, make it a habit to introduce yourself and follow-up with them, make them feel welcome. It's a sure way to make someone remember who you are.

66. Paid advertising. Research some influencers in your niche and find out if they offer advertising on their website. Most sites, if they have advertising options available, have an advertising link on their navigation bar so it's usually easy to know right away. Don't just research big influencers in your community; spend some time looking at other options – sites that your target market would also hang out at. For example if you're a weight loss coach, you could advertise on a site that is about self-help. One of the most common forms of advertisement website owner's offer is a 125 x 125 button they'll place in their sidebar.

67. Craigslist. When you think of Craigslist you probably think of buying or selling things on a local level. Most people don't think of it as a marketing platform for their business. But it can be. If you're hosting an in person event, promote it through the Craigslist event listings option. If you're not doing an event, but have a digital product you'd like to sell, create an ad. Make a plan for how you'll use Craigslist as a marketing tool. Don't just go in and create a bunch of ads. Be creative and think about the areas you want to market to. And remember, they also have a strict no spam policy so make sure you're following their rules when setting up your ads.

68. Classified ads - online. This tends to be something a lot of marketers don't think about or overlook. You can use sites like http://dir.yahoo.com/business/ Submit classified ads to market a new product or service you've just released, a giveaway you're doing, etc.

69. Classified ads – offline/local. You can also use your local newspapers to post classified ads. Use it to promote a new service or product you're offering. Create an ad to promote signing up for your newsletter. If you're hosting a giveaway or contest, create an ad for that. Don't forget to track your results. It's always important to know what kind of ROI you are getting on your efforts!

70. Giveaway old books and magazines. Instead of just throwing out old magazines you have, why not donate them? And before you drop them off at a local doctor's office (or library, dentist, etc.), make sure that you have a label on there with your business information listed. This way anyone who picks it up might see that and want to check out your website. Do the same thing for old books you're going to donate.

71. Affiliate program. One of the 'easiest' ways to market your business is by offering an affiliate program so that others earn a commission if someone purchases through their link. Make it even easier for them to do the marketing for you – create some affiliate tools and resources (ready-to-go emails, Facebook posts, Tweets, etc.) so they can just add their affiliate link and then share it.

72. Apparel. Have a shirt designed with your business logo or website information on it. When you're out in public wear the shirt and market without even thinking about it. There are other alternatives to a shirt, too. You can have baseball caps made, sweatshirts, scarves, book bags, coffee mugs (although that doesn't fall under apparel), and more. Get creative! Give them to family and friends and have them wear your marketing message, too.

73. Email signature. Every day millions of emails are sent. You probably spend a lot of time emailing with customers and potential customers. So don't forget the email signature line. This is valuable online real estate. Include a link to your website, your contact information, invite them to connect with you on social media, sign-up for your list and more.

74. Speak at a local networking event. Public speaking isn't on everyone's to-do list and if you're afraid of doing it, you're not alone. It's one of the most common fears people have. But, if you have the opportunity to showcase your expertise by speaking at a networking event, get up there and do it. One of the quickest ways to show people you're an expert in your niche is by being invited to speak at an event. And once the talk is over, you'll be able to have face-to-face conversations with potential customers and interact with others. And honestly, there's nothing better than in-person networking!

75. Host a giveaway. People like winning things so why not host some sort of giveaway on your site? Maybe you'll have something for first, second and third place. But don't forget everyone else that participates too. Maybe give away a free report to everyone.

Giveaways create a lot of buzz so it's an easy way to market your business.

76. Make a slideshow. Slideshows are a way to give your audience another way to learn from you. Remember, not everyone learns the same way so the more ways you can give people to consume your content, the better. With sites like Slideshare, (http://www.slideshare.net/) you have a platform to easily share a slide show presentation as well as all sorts of other content such as videos and PDFs just to name a few. The point here is to make sure that the information you share is branded with your business name.

77. QR code. In today's technologically advanced world, more and more people use smart phones. This gives you the opportunity to market in a whole new way – with QR codes. You've probably seen one before. They are little black and white square boxes that you scan with your mobile device. Essentially a QR code is a shortcut. Instead of someone having to type a URL into their browser, they can simply scan one of these and it will take them to the website, Facebook page – whatever the person has set the code up to do.

Try it out and see how it goes. Set one up to send people to your mailing list opt-in landing page (you do have one of those right?), your Facebook page, whatever – just test out this marketing option and see what happens.

You can quickly and easily create QR codes by using sites like QR Code Generator (http://goqr.me/) or KAYWA QR Code (http://qrcode.kaywa.com/), just to name a few. Note: if you're going to use QR codes, please make sure that whatever URL you are pointing someone too is optimized to be viewed on a mobile device!

78. Solo email advertisement. Another valuable way to market your business is to purchase a solo email mailing. You'll have to spend some time researching this one. Find others in your niche market and reach out to them to see if they offer the option to purchase a solo ad to be sent out in one of their newsletters/mailings. Keep in mind, a lot of people are very protective of their lists (as they should be and you should be too!) and are cautious of doing things like this especially if they don't know who you are or what your product is. This is why it's a good idea to build some sort of social media relationship with them and join their mailing list too.

79. Amazon reviews. Did you know you can set up an Amazon profile and edit it to include a picture of you, a brief description about you, a link to your website and more? This is an easy way to market your business. Once you have the profile set up you can spend 20 minutes a day leaving reviews for books you've read and items you've purchased. Why? Because when you do, if people see your comment and are interested in learning more about you, they can click on your name and it will take them to your Amazon profile.

80. Local business reviews. After you visit a local hair dresser, restaurant, retail store, etc. find out if they are listed anywhere online that you can write a review. The purpose of taking the time to write a review? While you're helping others by sharing your experience (a lot of people make a decision to visit a place by the reviews they read), you're also doing a little marketing for yourself by putting your name/information on the review.

81. Twitter lists. Set up a list in Twitter (you can make it public or private) and add influencers in your target market. These are the "gurus" you want to keep an eye on and see what they're up to, the leading experts. Share their content once in a while and just stay up to date on new things they're doing, what's working for them and what's not. You can learn a lot from those that are further ahead in business than you are so pay attention.

As you can see from this list, marketing your business can be done in as little as 20 minutes a day. The key takeaway is that you have to consistently market your business. It's all about putting a little effort into it each and every day to get your name out there, build relationships with those around you and showcase your expertise.

82. Live support on Periscope. Getting the same support ticket with no solution. Somethings are just too difficult to explain over the phone? Live-stream your support to your existing clients and answer numerous questions in one hit. Just 20 minutes of live streaming could really impress your clients to support you even more. So make sure to help them through the questionable areas of your products and services. Your clients will fall in love with you all over again!

Disclaimer

This book has been written for information purposes only. Every effort has been made to make this book as complete and accurate as possible. However, there may be mistakes in typography or content. Also, this book provides information only up to the publishing date. Therefore, this book should be used as a guide - not as the ultimate source.

The purpose of this book is to educate. The author and the publisher does not warrant that the information contained in this book is fully complete and shall not be responsible for any errors or omissions. The author and publisher shall have neither liability nor responsibility to any person or entity with respect to any loss or damage caused or alleged to be caused directly or indirectly by this book.

ABOUT THE AUTHOR

T. Ray Greer, Jr. literally consumes any and everything related to news, documentaries and books dealing with current events, politics, history and business. He's thankful to have the responsibility to teach such a wide variety of content, because it exposes him to a wealth of knowledge. This very knowledge creates a sense of excitement as he shares it with each and every person that he comes in contact with in the world.

Mr. Greer is a graduate of Victory University with a Bachelor of Science degree in Christian Ministry. He's the pastor of Salem Baptist Church in Mason, TN. He also serves as the President of Greerology LLC in Memphis, TN.

Mr. Greer is a very tech savvy person that loves to do graphic design, cement contracting, blogging and website development.

He's happily married to his wonderful wife, Demetria. They also have a son affectionately called Trey.

www.ingramcontent.com/pod-product-compliance
Lightning Source LLC
Chambersburg PA
CBHW070746180526
45168CB00004B/1550